THIS

SUPERHERO HANDBOOK

BELONGS TO

Tobios

Greene

For Oonágh

With special thanks to "The Researchables,"
Conall, Erin, and Cara, for their meticulous
research work.

And for Arali and Stanley—
the dynamic duo.

Published in 2017 by
Laurence King Publishing Ltd
361–373 City Road, London,
EC1V 1LR, United Kingdom
T +44 (0)20 7841 6900
F + 44 (0)20 7841 6910
enquiries@laurenceking.com
www.laurenceking.com

This book was produced by Laurence King Publishing Ltd, London

A catalog record for this book is available from the British Library

ISBN: 978-1-78067-974-7

Printed in China

THE SUPERHERO HANDBOOK

JAMES DOYLE & JASON FORD

LAURENCE KING PUBLISHING

CONTENTS

ATTENTION SUPERHEROES!

SOME SUPERHERO ACTIVITIES REQUIRE HELP FROM YOUR ADULT ALLIES. ALWAYS LET A PARENT OR GUARDIAN KNOW BEFORE YOU BEGIN A CHALLENGE.

DEAR ASPIRING SUPERHERO,

Now that you have picked up this book, there is no turning back. Your life as an ordinary civilian is over. Having started to read these pages, you have placed yourself squarely into the world of the superhero—a world that requires great courage, great knowledge and great responsibility.

Would you like to join the forces of good in the fight against evil? If the answer to this question is "Yes," then you have taken your first step into the heart-pounding, super-powered, and adrenalin-filled world of the superhero.

When your superhero call comes, you must be ready. This handbook will help prepare you for the challenges ahead.

Find your superhero name, identify your superpower, and learn how to be a good superhero. Then create your own superhero outfit and gadgets, choose your secret hideout, and design your superhero transport. Finally, test and practice your superpowers. Then you will be ready for anything the bad guys might throw at you!

This book will not only keep you one step ahead of the world's baddies … it might just help you

save the planet! If you are too scared, then put this book right back where you found it. But if you think you have the nerve to become a superhero, then this is the book for you.

SIGN THE SUPERHERO OATH ON THE NEXT PAGE AND LET'S GET STARTED!

SIGN THE
SUPERHERO OATH

**It is essential that the teachings and ways of the
superhero remain secret from ordinary civilians.
The knowledge held within this handbook is
far too dangerous in untrained hands.**

The first step in your superhero training is to sign the Superhero
Oath. Once signed, you are bound to the rules of a superhero as laid
down by BLAST (Board of Legislation Against Superhero Treason).
Failure to comply with the superhero rules will result in BLAST
stripping you of your superhero status, name, costume, powers,
and all other superhero equipment.

SUPERHERO
OATH

I, _Tobias_, SWEAR I WILL BE LOYAL AND SHOW TOTAL ALLEGIANCE TO THE WAYS AND TEACHINGS OF THE SUPERHERO. I WILL DUTIFULLY FOLLOW THESE WAYS AND TEACHINGS IN MY ENDEAVOR TO COMBAT ALL WRONG-DOING AND PROMOTE PEACE AND HARMONY ON THE STREETS. I PROMISE TO KEEP MY SUPERHERO IDENTITY SECRET.

SIGNED _Tobias Green_

DATE _Thursday_

B.L.A.S.T

FIND YOUR
SUPERHERO NAME

A superhero needs a super name. Nobody will take you seriously as a superpower without a cool name.

Imagine arriving at the scene of a crime and announcing yourself as Mop Man or Window Woman. It certainly won't strike fear into your enemy. Use the first letter of your first name and the first letter of your last name to find your superhero name!

FIRST NAME INITIAL

A	Night
B	Agent
C	Silver
D	Fantastic
E	Aqua
F	Steel
G	Captain
H	Silent
I	Phantom
J	Space
K	Gold
L	Magnificent
M	Invisible
N	Scarlet
O	Fire
P	Galactic
Q	Star
R	Professor
S	Time
(T)	Mind
U	Super
V	Thunder
W	Doctor
X	Swamp
Y	Green
Z	Shadow

LAST NAME INITIAL

A	Hawk
B	Cape
C	Wonder
D	Streak
E	Blaze
F	Guardian
G	Striker
H	Skull
I	Hunter
J	Arrow
K	Mask
L	Knight
M	Boy/Girl
N	Ghost
O	Shield
P	Bolt
Q	Hammer
R	Raven
S	Light
(T)	Fist
U	Blade
V	Crusader
W	Hope
X	Titan
Y	Justice
Z	Thing

MY SUPERHERO NAME IS

Minde Fist

FIND YOUR
SUPERPOWER

Whether we like to admit it or not, all of us have a talent for something.

You might be brilliant at computer games or really good at sports. Or you could be a math genius or have the ability to speak another language. Regardless of your talent, this is the first step in discovering where your superpowers lie.

Make a list of the things you are good at, then think about how these skills and talents could be molded into a superpower.

MATCH THE TALENT OR SKILL ON THE LEFT WITH THE SUPERPOWER ON THE RIGHT

YOUR TALENT OR SKILL

YOUR SUPERPOWER

1: Good planner / well organized

2: Strong / athletic / good at sports

3: Good at games / good with technology / likes computers

4: Brave / cool and calm under pressure / doesn't get nervous

5: Good cyclist / skateboarder / gymnast

6: Clever but quiet / likes to blend into a crowd

A: Super strength or super speed

B: Ice cool— able to freeze any object

C: Invisibility

D: Incredible agility and jumping ability

E: Can disable any electrical / security / computer system

F: Mind control or hypnotism

ANSWERS: 1F • 2A • 3E • 4B • 5D • 6C

CHOOSE YOUR
SIDEKICK

Some superheroes prefer to go it alone and live a solitary life of brooding mystery. For them this is a convenient and uncomplicated life of saving the planet without having to worry about anybody else. Others choose to have a sidekick— someone to watch their back and ideally have skills to cover for their weaknesses.

WHO TO CHOOSE?

Your sidekick needs to be up to the job and someone you can trust with everything. Write down the names of three people you would trust in a situation where your life depended on it. It could be a relative, a best friend, a team mate, or even a pet.

Name 1: _Cece_

Name 2: _Logan_

Name 3: _Lucas_

Once you've found some suitable candidates, use the Superhero Sidekick Application Form to record key information about your potential partner in crime-fighting. What skills and talents does your potential sidekick have, and how do they fit in with your own superpowers? Most importantly, do you really "click" together? Once you're satisfied you've got the right sidekick, then you are officially a deadly duo!

SUPERHERO
SIDEKICK
APPLICATION FORM

REAL NAME ~~Tobias~~ Nibde Fist

SIDEKICK ALIAS Logan, Lubas lele

WHAT IS YOUR SUPERPOWER? invisibility

WHAT SIDEKICK QUALITIES DO YOU HAVE?

- ☑ SKILLS THIS SUPERHERO LACKS
- ☑ TRUSTWORTHINESS
- ☐ LOYALTY
- ☐ NEVER GIVING IN
- ☑ GOOD TIMING
- ☐ HATING BAD GUYS

B.L.A.S.T

HOW TO BE A
GOOD SUPERHERO

With the superhero role comes great responsibility, and there are certain key characteristics that you must have if you are to be a success.

BE ASSURED

A top superhero will stand tall and confident (without being arrogant). He or she will speak clearly and make good eye contact with each member of the public and any members of your superhero team. The key is for people to be at ease with you but also believe in you to get the job done.

BE YOURSELF

Even though, as a superhero, you have to keep your real identity secret, always stay true to yourself. Pretending to be someone you are not will begin to show after a while and people will soon lose trust in you.

BE POSITIVE

Try to be positive with anyone you have dealings with. Praise will help to keep people's spirits up, while negativity will quickly erode morale.

5 Quickly and carefully use the tongs to lift the very hot can. Turn it completely upside down and place it in the saucepan of cold water.

KRUNCH!

6 Watch as the can is crushed immediately, right before your very eyes.

SUPERHERO SECRET

Heating the can caused the water inside it to boil. The water vapour from the boiling water forced the air inside the can out of it. Once the can was filled with water vapour and then suddenly cooled, the water vapour within the can condensed and created a vacuum. This vacuum inside the can made it easy for the pressure of the air outside the can to crush it without your help.

DESIGN YOUR SUPERHERO SYMBOL

Your superhero symbol should make you instantly recognizable. It needs to adorn everything related to you, from your costume to your call sign, from your secret hideout to your superhero gadgets.

EXPRESS YOURSELF

It is essential that your symbol captures exactly what your superhero identity is about. For example, if your identity is related to an animal, such as a cat, then model your design on the physical features of that animal—say, a cat's paw or ears. If your identity is related to a natural force, such as a storm, then chose an appropriate representation—a lightning bolt, for instance.

CHOOSE COLORS CAREFULLY

Keep colors in your symbol consistent. Don't have too many— try sticking to one or two bold colors. The colors in your symbol will need to work closely with the design of your superhero outfit.

KEEP LETTERING SIMPLE

Try not to overdo the wording on your symbol—you want something short, snappy, and catchy. Better yet, use just one letter from your superhero name.

USE THIS SPACE TO DESIGN YOUR VERY OWN SUPERHERO SYMBOL

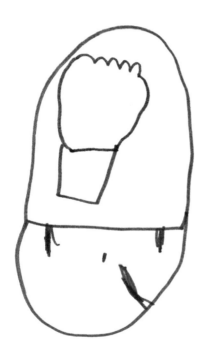

INSTRUCTIONS

1 Fill the saucepan with cold water.

2 Put a tablespoon of water inside the drink can.

3 Now heat the can on the stove to boil the water inside.

4 When the water is boiled, a little cloud of condensation will rise out of the top of the can.

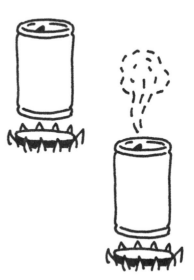

● Once you have mastered defying gravity with one ball, practise until you can control two, three or even more!

The moving hot air from the hair dryer pushes the ping-pong ball up with a force equal to the force of gravity. Also, air pressure creates a column of air in which the ping-pong ball is held, making it easier to control the movement of the ball. The tougher test is to control two, three or even more ping-pong balls all at once. Practice will allow you to defy the force of gravity like a superhero!

MAKE A SUPERHERO SHIELD

Use everyday items
to create the perfect
superhero protection device—
a shield. Many of our best-known
superheroes have used a shield
in their adventures. Once you have
assembled your shield, personalize it with
your very own superhero colors and your new
superhero name!

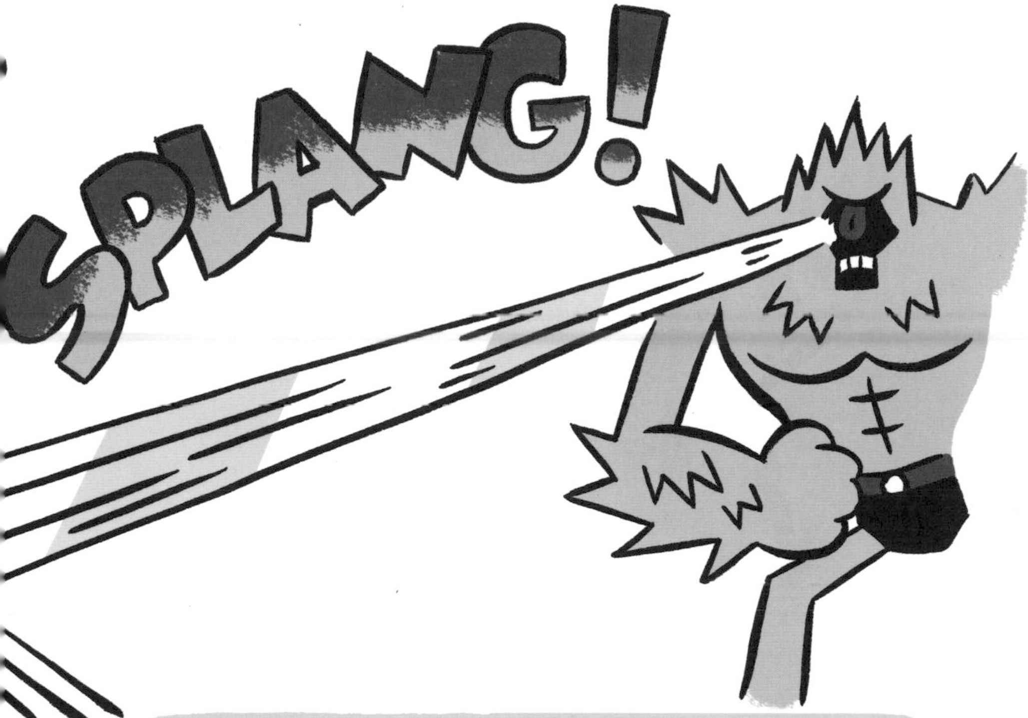
SPLANG!

MATERIALS

MEASURING TAPE

LARGE PIECE OF CORRUGATED CARDBOARD

SCISSORS

BELT

ALUMINUM FOIL

GLUE

INSTRUCTIONS

1. Take the hair dryer and plug it in. Turn it on to the lowest and coolest setting.

2. Hold the hair dryer so that it is pointing straight up in the air.

3. Set your ping-pong ball directly above the current of air coming out of the hair dryer. What happens?

4 Start with the bottom two slits. Slowly thread the belt up through the bottom slit and back through the top slit, making sure that the belt runs along the back of the shield where you can slide your arm through, and then thread it through the two remaining slits at the top of the shield. Fasten the belt by buckling it as you would if you were fastening it on yourself.

BELT

5 Finally, take your aluminum foil and glue it to the shield so that the outside of the shield is completely covered. Personalize the shield by adding other materials to decorate it in your superhero colors or symbols, or cut out your superhero name or initials from the foil.

FOIL

SUPERHERO
SECRET

The measuring you did was critical to getting the perfect shield for your size— too big a shield is actually a hindrance as you will not be able to see past it, and as you tire it will slow you down. Too small a shield for your body size will offer you little or no protection. Imagine trying to hide a grizzly bear behind a matchstick!

MAKE AN
INVISIBILITY
MIRROR

If you're lucky enough to have the superpower of invisibility you won't need this activity as ... well ... you're already invisible! But if not, this very simple experiment uses clever super science to make you vanish into thin air.

BEFORE

MATERIALS

LARGE FLAT AREA
TO WORK IN

1 PERSON/SUPERHERO

SCISSORS

1 PIECE OF
ALUMINUM FOIL
12IN LONG

TZAM!!

AFTER

INSTRUCTIONS

12IN

1 Unroll the aluminum foil over a flat area.

2 Estimate a length of foil around 12in. Take the scissors and cut the foil from the roll.

3 Hold your piece of foil up in the air in front of you. Turn it to inspect both sides. You will notice that one side of the foil is shinier than the other. Place your piece of foil down shiny side up.

4 Lean down over your piece of foil and you'll be able to see your reflection. (Unless you have the power of invisibility, of course.) Now lift the foil and gently scrunch it up in your hands—but not too much or you'll rip and tear it, and need to start all over again.

5 Place the piece of foil back on the ground and flatten it out a little so that it looks fairly flat but still has some tiny bumps and crease lines (just as a scrunched piece of paper might look after it has been flattened out again).

6 Lean down over your piece of foil again. What happened? You've vanished!

SUPERHERO SECRET

On the flat, smooth piece of foil, light rays bounce back off the surface in a perfectly straight line, allowing you to see your image in exactly the same way you would in a mirror. The crumpled piece of foil, however, is a mass of uneven lumps, bumps, and crease lines. This causes the light rays to bounce around in many random, different directions and prevents your proper mirror image from forming.

MAKE
GIANT SMASH 'EM HANDS

Some super-strong superheroes have mighty big hands that help them clobber bad guys. You can create super-sized hands of your own.

MATERIALS

½ CUP OF VINEGAR

1 DISPOSABLE LATEX GLOVE
(SUPERHEROES WITH A
LATEX INTOLERANCE
NEED TO USE
NON-LATEX GLOVES)

¼ CUP OF BAKING SODA

1 SUPER-RELIABLE
SIDEKICK

WARNING! This activity can get very messy and is best done outside or over a sink or bathtub.

INSTRUCTIONS

1 Have your trusty sidekick hold the glove over the sink with the fingers pointing down and the glove opening held wide open.

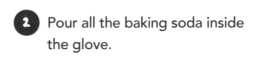

2 Pour all the baking soda inside the glove.

3 Now pour all the vinegar into the glove and very quickly close the glove opening. Keep it tightly closed so no air can get in.

● Hold the glove like that for a few minutes and see what pops up! If you've held it super tight and no gas escapes, the glove inflates like a balloon and blows up like a super-sized hand of a superhero. Then it will begin to return to normal size.

SUPERHERO SECRET

The mixture of the baking soda and vinegar generates carbon dioxide gas in the glove. As the reaction takes off, the glove is inflated into a super-sized hand before the reaction fizzes out and the glove returns to normal size again.

DESIGN A
UTILITY BELT

Not all superheroes use utility belts, choosing to rely on their superpowers, but they can be very useful for carrying super supplies that you might need while fighting bad guys. You may find that it is one of the most important parts of your superhero outfit.

You can use a utility belt to carry portable devices for slowing down baddies, tools for investigating crime, and gadgets to help you move around stealthily.

MICRO TORCH

SAT NAV

IMMOBILIZING
GUNK

HOLES

FIRST AID
KIT

HIDDEN
CAMERA

USE THE SPACES BELOW TO DRAW THE SUPER SUPPLIES YOU NEED IN YOUR UTILITY BELT

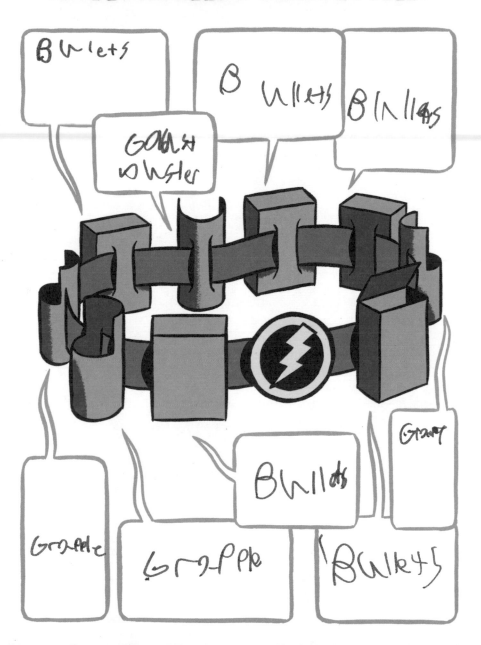

SUPER ACTIVITY

MAKE A
UTILITY BELT

Having a utility belt makes it easier to carry super supplies around with you. Be ready at any moment with gadgets to help you fight crime and make life difficult for bad guys!

QUICK! ONE OF MY INSTANT HOLES!

MATERIALS

 BELT (ASK MOM OR DAD BEFORE USING ONE OF THEIRS!)

**CARDBOARD TUBES
(LIKE YOU FIND IN PAPER TOWELS)**

 **SMALL CARDBOARD BOXES
(LIKE IN A CEREAL VARIETY PACK)**

1 PIECE OF FLAT CARDBOARD

SCISSORS

STICKY TAPE

 **ALUMINUM FOIL**

PAINT

INSTRUCTIONS

1 Make capsules, pockets, and a buckle cover for your utility belt.

CAPSULE Cut the cardboard tubes to the size you want your capsules to be. Now cut partway down a tube from the top edge. Make a cut the same length on the other side of the tube, then cut across to the bottom of the first cut to remove a section of the tube. In the back of the tube, cut two vertical slits. Make sure the slits are long enough that your belt will fit through them. Cover the bottom of the tube with cardboard to seal it closed, or leave it open to use as a holster for a ray gun or other super gadget!

CUT

CUT

BELT

POCKET Take a small cardboard box. Leave the largest flap on the top of the box, and cut the other flaps off. On the back of the box, cut two vertical slits. Make sure the slits are long enough that your belt will fit through them.

BUCKLE COVER On a piece of flat cardboard draw an oval, square, or any other shape you like, making sure your buckle cover is taller than your belt. Cut a slit near the left and right edges of your buckle cover. Make sure the slits are long enough that your belt and its buckle will fit through them.

2 Cover your capsules, pockets, and buckle cover with aluminum foil, decorate them with your superhero symbol, or paint them in your superhero colors! Leave them to dry.

3 Thread your belt through both slits in your buckle cover. Then slide your canisters and pockets onto your belt. Fasten the belt and slide your buckle cover around until it sits over the buckle on your belt. Now load up your utility belt with super supplies!

SUPERHERO
SECRET

Since Ancient Greek and Roman times, soldiers have used belts to carry weapons and supplies, so they can keep their hands free. Belts also help transfer weight from your back or shoulders to your hips, letting your strong leg muscles take care of any heavy lifting. This also lowers your center of gravity, helping to keep you stable while fighting bad guys on rough terrain!

MAKE
IMMOBILIZING
GUNK

Use slimy immobilizing gunk to slow down bad guys, or just to mess with during your superhero downtime. You can make your slime any color you like—from disgusting booger green to radioactive pink.

MATERIALS

1 JUG OF WARM WATER

LAUNDRY GEL

FOOD COLORING OF YOUR CHOICE

WHITE GLUE

2 LARGE BOWLS

1 CUP AND SOME SPOONS

INSTRUCTIONS

LAUNDRY GEL

WARM WATER

1 Pour 17 fl oz of warm water into one of the bowls.

2 Mix in 1 fl oz of laundry gel and leave the mixture to cool a little.

FOOD COLORING

WARM WATER

WHITE GLUE

3 In the other bowl, mix three spoonfuls of water with two spoonfuls of white glue. Now add a few drops of food coloring and mix until you are happy with the color.

- Take a spoonful of the laundry gel mixture and add it to the glue and food coloring. Mix well. You've just made immobilizing gunk … enjoy!

The proteins and sugars in your slimy gunk have similar characteristics to those made by your body—they work and act in the same way as, for example, snot or boogers. They are sticky substances that gather along stretchable strings called "protein strands." If you've got your mixtures right, you should have colored, stringy-stretchy gunk.

MAKE
SUPER STINK
BOMBS

**Use super stink bombs to disperse a crowd of criminals.
Clear a crime scene as quickly as you can say KA-POW!**

MATERIALS

4 EGGS

FUNNEL

1 GLASS JAR
WITH A SCREW-TOP LID

1 PACKAGE OF
WATER BALLOONS

WATER

WARNING! This activity is very smelly and best done outdoors.
Check with a parent or guardian before beginning.

INSTRUCTIONS

1 Take your four eggs and crack them into the glass jar.

2 Tighten the lid and set the eggs on a window ledge for two full days. Ideally, choose a window that gets a lot of sunlight. This will help speed the rotting process.

3 From time to time, check the jar and sniff the eggs for that rotten-egg smell.

4 When you're happy that the smell is just right, take the funnel and set it into the opening of one of your water balloons.

AARGH!

5 Now fill the water balloon about halfway full with the eggs. Fill the rest of the balloon with water and tie the end tight. Then bombs away! You've just made a smelly addition to your armory.

SUPERHERO SECRET

When eggs go bad, bacteria breaks down the egg protein. This process produces a chemical called hydrogen sulfide—the source of that distinctive "rotten-egg smell." Making super stink bombs will not cause any major health hazard to you and other humans, but breathing in sulfur-based gases is a bad idea. Also, make sure you don't eat any of the rotten egg mix—it will make you quite ill and very un-super!

DESIGN SOME
SUPERHERO GADGETS

Gadgets are essential for a superhero's everyday work and survival. Here are some simple tips for designing your own gadgets.

PERSONALIZE IT!

Your gadgets must suit your personal requirements and should also fit your superpower. What use is an ice blaster if your superpower is fire? Why make gadgets waterproof if you can't swim? And what if your gadgets are made for a left-handed superhero and you are right-handed?

NAME IT!

The best superhero gadgets are not just known for what they do, but also for how they are named. Start by thinking about what sort of device your gadget is: "meter" at the end of a word means a device for measuring things. "Graph" means a device for recording or transmitting information. Sonar devices use sound to detect and locate objects. Now add some superhero power to your gadget name! For example: Blast-o-meter, Mega-graph, Stealth-sonar.

USE THIS SPACE TO DESIGN YOUR OWN SUPER GADGET

SUPER ACTIVITY

MAKE AN IMPROVISED FIRE EXTINGUISHER

Fires can be very dangerous, even to crime fighters. Although most crime fighters are based in cities, they are not always guaranteed to have a fire station close by or instant access to water or a fire extinguisher. With just some basic household items, however, you can save the day with your super skills and fire-fighting know-how.

WARNING! If you want to test your fire extinguisher on a fire (even a tiny one), adult supervision is essential!

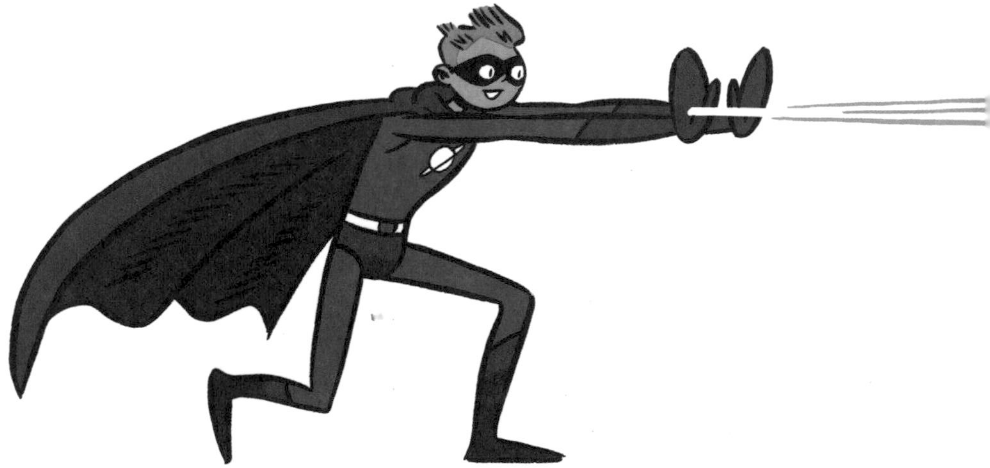

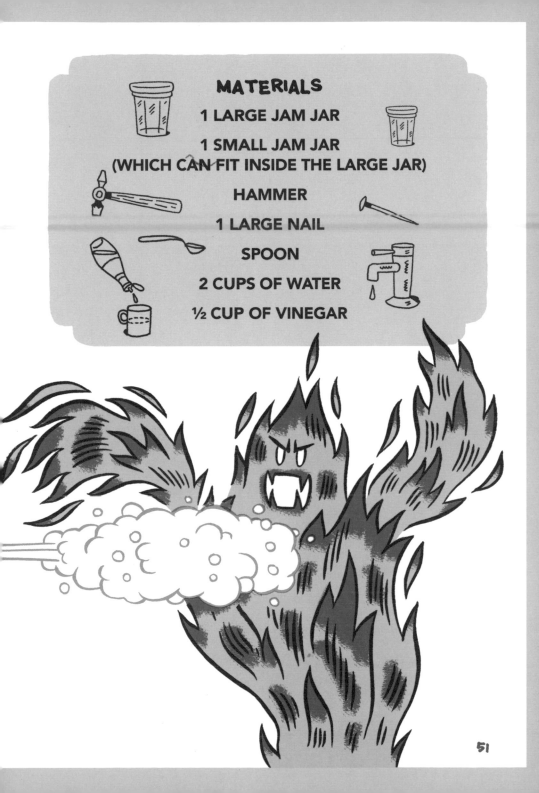

MATERIALS
1 LARGE JAM JAR

1 SMALL JAM JAR
(WHICH CAN FIT INSIDE THE LARGE JAR)

HAMMER

1 LARGE NAIL

SPOON

2 CUPS OF WATER

½ CUP OF VINEGAR

INSTRUCTIONS

1. Place the lid of the large jam jar flat on a workbench or outside table. Next, take the hammer and nail and make a hole in the lid.

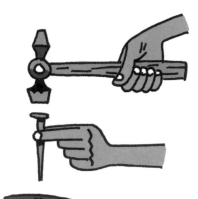

2. Take the 2 cups of water and pour them into the large jam jar.

3. Stir the baking soda into the large jar of water.

4. Take the ½ cup of vinegar and pour it into the small jar. Then carefully place the small jar (without a lid) into the large jar without spilling any vinegar at all.

5. Finally, tightly screw the lid of the large jam jar (the one you made a hole in) back on. Turn the jar away from you and towards the fire. A foamy substance should start to fly from the hole of the jar lid and help put out the fire.

One of the essential ingredients needed for a fire to burn is oxygen. Without it, fires start to die out. As you mix the vinegar in the small jar with the baking soda in the large one, the vinegar reacts with the baking soda (also called sodium bicarbonate), and this chemical reaction creates carbon dioxide gas, which smothers the fire and stops it from getting oxygen.

MAKE AN
ELECTRO-
MAGNET

An electro-magnet allows you to move metal objects around at will—a very cool and useful tool for any self-respecting superhero. Let's get magnetizing!

MATERIALS

 1 LARGE IRON NAIL ABOUT 3IN LONG

ABOUT 3FT OF THINLY COATED COPPER WIRE

 1 NEW 1.5 VOLT D-TYPE BATTERY

STICKY TAPE

PAPER CLIPS, PINS, OR OTHER SMALL METAL OBJECTS

INSTRUCTIONS

1 Take your nail and coated wire. Wrap most of the wire around the nail, leaving about 7 or 8in of wire free at either end (you need the wire at the ends to hook your nail up to the battery). Try not to overlap the wires.

2 Now remove about 1in of the plastic coating from both ends of the wire. Attach one end of the wire to one end of the battery and the other wire to the other end of the battery. It's best to tape the wires to the battery. Be careful, though—the wires can heat up!

3 Now you have your own electro-magnet. Place the point of the nail near a few paper clips or metal and see what happens!

Your electro-magnet uses up the electricity in the battery quite quickly, which is why the battery may get warm, so disconnect the wires when you are done with your super gadget.

Most magnets you will find cannot be turned off, like the magnets in refrigerators. Electro-magnets like the one you have made can be switched on and off when you add and remove electricity. Hence their name: electro-magnets. The electricity flowing through the wire arranges the molecules in the nail so that they are attracted to certain metals.

MAKE A
SUPERHERO
MEGA-BLASTER

All superheroes need a show-stopping skill or power to make people go "Wow! Awesome!" Follow these instructions to create the mega-blaster—an explosive fountain of foam that can reach as high as nine metres into the air.

WARNING! This activity is best performed outdoors unless you want to suffer a superhero's worst fate— the wrath of your parents!

MATERIALS

**1 LARGE BOTTLE OF COLA
(SOME SUPERHEROES SAY
DIET COLA WORKS BEST)**

½ PACKET OF SCOTCH MINTS

**KITCHEN FUNNEL OR TUBE
(NOT ESSENTIAL, BUT MAKES THE TRANSFER
OF MINTS TO COLA EASIER)**

INSTRUCTIONS

1 Place your large bottle of cola on a flat piece of ground or a stable surface like a board. Place it upright and unscrew the lid. If you have a funnel or tube, place it in the neck of the bottle.

2 Now drop the scotch mints into the cola and stand clear! If done correctly, you have just created a super blast of cola that will impress your superhero fans.

Carbon dioxide is the gas that makes soft drinks bubbly. The gas doesn't get released until you open the bottle. Even more if you shake it beforehand! Scotch mints are covered in tiny dimples—a bit like a golf ball is. These dramatically increase the surface area of the mint and encourage a huge number of bubbles to form on the mints. All of these factors combine to create a super-fast eruption of cola.

61

CHOOSE YOUR
SECRET HIDEOUT

All self-respecting superheroes have a secret base or hideaway where they can plan and carry out secret missions without exposure to the general public, the media, or, worse still, their evil nemesis. A secret hideout must meet certain criteria if it is going to be fit for a superhero.

HIDEOUT CHECKLIST

Look at this checklist of the key features of a secret hideout. Work through the list and grade your must-haves from 1 to 10 (1 being the most important and 10 being the least important).

- [ ] Secret escape hatch
- [ ] Heliport
- [ ] Chill-out room (for superhero downtime)
- [ ] Self-destruct button (if lair is discovered)
- [ ] High-tech security system
- [ ] Surveillance room
- [ ] Code-protected safe
- [ ] Costume/equipment room
- [ ] Laboratory
- [ ] Call-sign spotlight

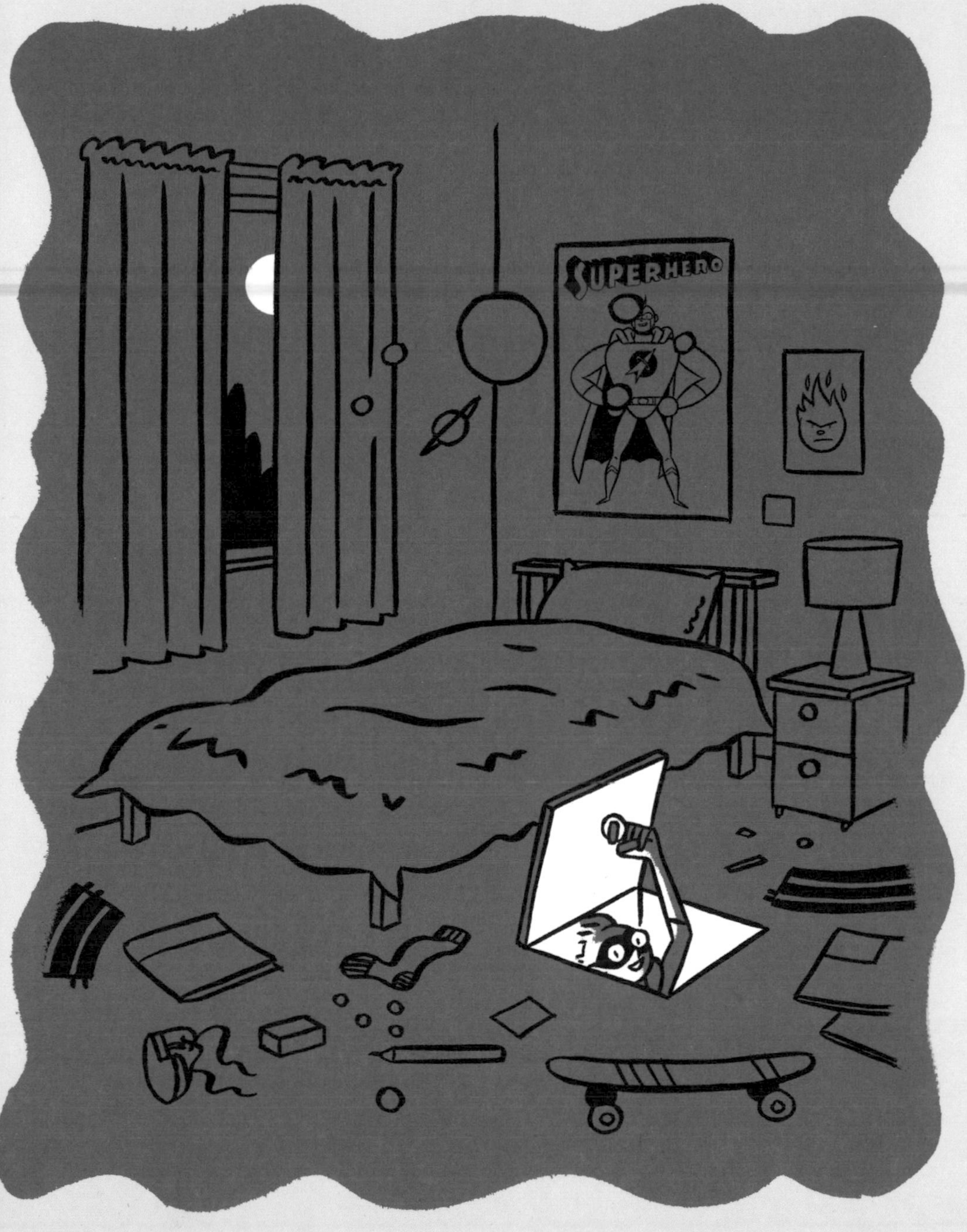
SUPERHERO

MAKE SUPERHERO SECRET CODES

Codes can help you keep your secret superhero information between you and your trusty sidekick or loyal best friend. Civilians and supervillains won't be able to read your coded messages, but with the right key, you and your team will be able to decipher them.

THE CLASSIC REVERSE ALPHABET

This is a straight-forward code to start with. Simply take the standard alphabet and reverse it so that A becomes Z, and so on.

Key:

A	B	C	D	E	F	G	H	I	J	K	L	M	N	O	P	Q	R	S	T	U	V	W	X	Y	Z
Z	Y	X	W	V	U	T	S	R	Q	P	O	N	M	L	K	J	I	H	G	F	E	D	C	B	A

Try it out:

NVVG ZG SRWVLFG

SEE PAGE 67 FOR ANSWERS!

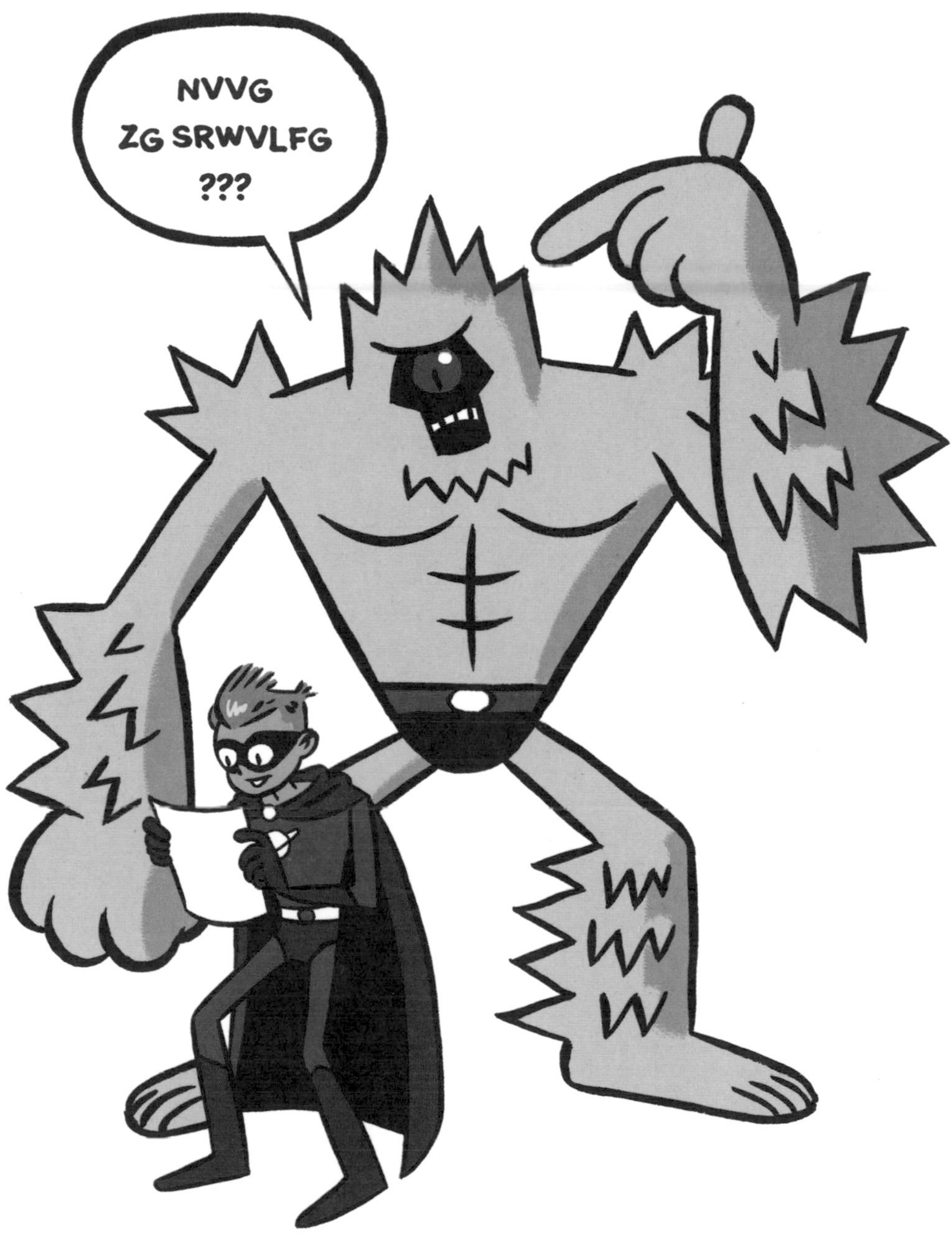
NVVG
ZG SRWVLFG
???

AUGUSTUS'S CODE

Augustus's code is very effective and uses one simple rule: you just substitute the next letter of the alphabet for the original one. In other words, A becomes B, B becomes C, and so on, right to the end of the alphabet, where Z then becomes A.

Key:

A	B	C	D	E	F	G	H	I	J	K	L	M	N	O	P	Q	R	S	T	U	V	W	X	Y	Z
B	C	D	E	F	G	H	I	J	K	L	M	N	O	P	Q	R	S	T	U	V	W	X	Y	Z	A

Try it out:

BUUBDL BU EVTL

REMEMBER!
ONLY SHARE YOUR CODES
WITH THOSE YOU TRUST
MOST, AND NEVER
REVEAL YOUR CODES
TO THE ENEMY.

NUMBER CODE

In this code, each letter of the alphabet is substituted for a number. ABC becomes 123 and so on, right up to Z, which is represented by 26. Note: Spacing is crucial between numbers as 26, for example, could be misread as 2 and 6. Write your number codes carefully.

Key:

A	B	C	D	E	F	G	H	I	J	K	L	M	N	O	P	Q	R	S	T	U	V	W	X	Y	Z
1	2	3	4	5	6	7	8	9	10	11	12	13	14	15	16	17	18	19	20	21	22	23	24	25	26

Try it out:

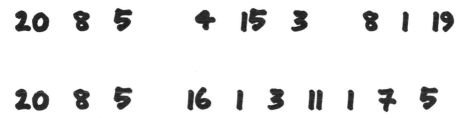

20 8 5   4 15 3   8 1 19

20 8 5   16 1 3 11 1 7 5

WRITE SUPER SECRET MESSAGES

This superhero skill will allow you to write secret messages and communicate with other superheroes without people knowing. Secret messages will disappear right in front of your eyes! You can plan and plot with those you know and trust, and keep those you don't completely in the dark.

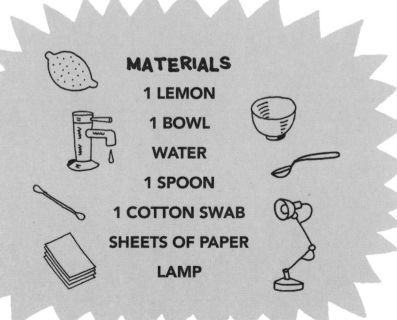

MATERIALS

1 LEMON

1 BOWL

WATER

1 SPOON

1 COTTON SWAB

SHEETS OF PAPER

LAMP

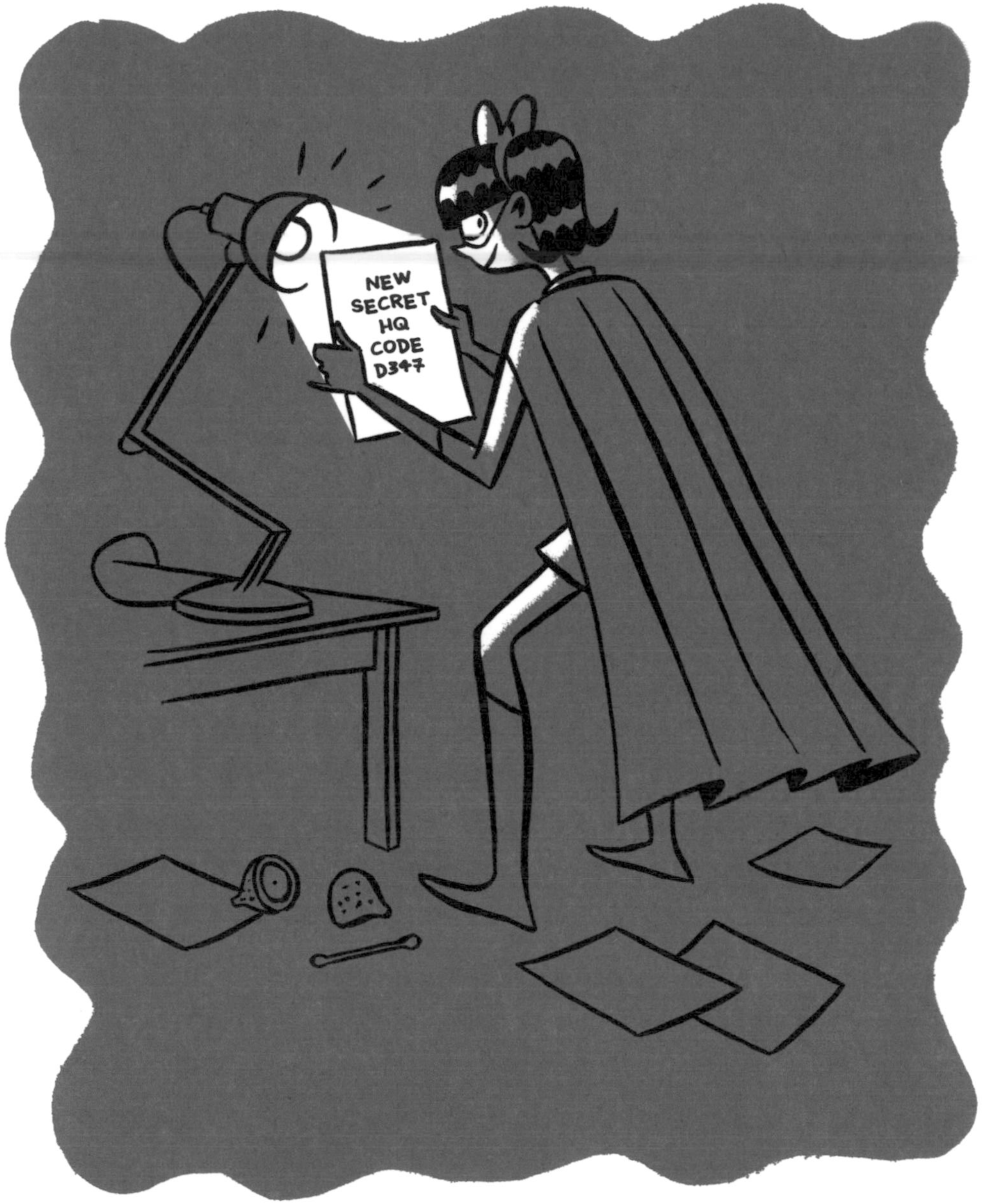
NEW SECRET HQ CODE D347

INSTRUCTIONS

1 Cut the lemon in half and squeeze both halves into the bowl.

2 Add a few drops of water to the lemon juice and stir with the spoon.

3 Dip the cotton swab into the water/lemon mixture.

4 Use the cotton swab on one of the sheets of paper to write a secret message.

5 As the message dries, it will disappear.

6 To read the message, hold the sheet of paper in front of a lamp. (Switch it on first.)

DESIGN YOUR
SUPERHERO
TRANSPORT

Whatever your superpower, you will need a few specialized super vehicles to help with your day-to-day planet-saving duties. Even if you can move at super speeds, superheroes need transport for several reasons.

ADDITIONAL PROTECTION

A tank or armored car with heat-seeking rockets just makes the task of defeating bad guys that little bit easier.

LESS EQUIPMENT TO LUG AROUND

If you can whisk yourself around in a super submersible, rocket, or helicopter, you can carry and store extra equipment and weaponry you would otherwise have to carry on your person.

LOOKING COOL

Superhero rockets, bikes, and cars look really cool and are fitted out with some amazing stuff. These vehicles will not only help you fight crime, but also add to your superhero image.

USE THIS SPACE TO DESIGN YOUR ULTIMATE SUPER VEHICLE

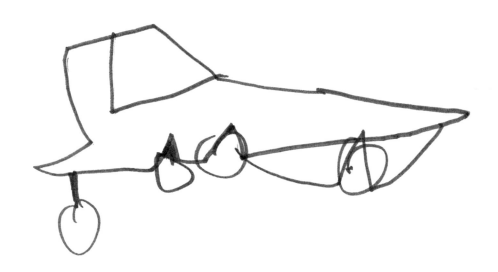

MAKE A
MINI HOVER
BOARD

Discover how to fight the force of
gravity and create a mini version
of the hover boards used by
some superheroes.

MATERIALS

 STICKY TAPE

1 PIN OR SMALL NAIL

 1 OLD CD OR DVD

1 9IN BALLOON

1 PULL-UP CAP FROM A WASHING-UP BOTTLE OR A WATER BOTTLE

HOT GLUE GUN OR STRONG GLUE THAT WILL BOND PLASTICS (LIKE AMAZING GOOP®)

WARNING! Be sure to get a parent or guardian's help with the hot glue gun or strong glue.

INSTRUCTIONS

1 Cover the center hole of the CD or DVD with a piece of tape and poke about six holes in the tape with a pin or small nail. This slows down the flow of air and allows your hover board to hover longer.

2 Use the hot glue gun or strong glue to stick the cap to the center of the CD or DVD. Create a good seal to keep air from escaping. Let the glue set.

3 Blow up the balloon all the way and pinch the neck—do not tie it!

4 Make sure the pop-up top is closed, then fit the neck of the balloon over the pop-up portion of the cap. (You may need a sidekick to help!)

HIIISSSS!

5 When you're ready to start hovering, simply put the hover board on a smooth surface and pop the top open.

SUPERHERO SECRET

The air coming out of the balloon causes a cushion of moving air between the disk and the surface. This lifts the disk and reduces the friction between the disk and the surface, which allows the disk to hover freely—just like a superhero hover board!

MAKE A
MINI JET PACK

Using the simple elements of air and pressure, plus a few basic materials, you can build your very own miniaturized super-powered jet pack.

MATERIALS

 1 PIECE OF STRING ABOUT 20FT LONG

 1 STRAW

 STICKY TAPE

 **1 BALLOON**

 **1 SUPER SIDEKICK TO HELP**

INSTRUCTIONS

1 Get your sidekick to take one end of the string and attach it to something strong like a tree or a fence.

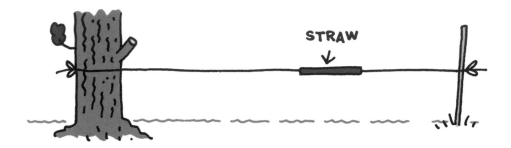

STRAW

2 Run the other end of the string through the straw and tie the end to another object so the string is nice and tight.

3 Now inflate the balloon but don't tie it (the air needs to escape for your jet pack to fly).

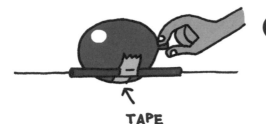

4 Hold the end of the balloon and get your trusty sidekick to tape the straw to the side of the balloon.

TAPE

WHOOOSH!

5 When you're ready, let the balloon go and watch your mini jet pack in action!

SUPERHERO
SECRET

Wind is caused by air moving from places that are under high pressure to places under lower pressure. The air inside the balloon or mini jet pack is under much greater pressure than the air outside the balloon. As you let go of the balloon, the air inside is forced out very, very quickly and this creates a thrust, which forces your jet pack forward.

TEST YOUR SUPER-POWERS

Now that you have your superhero name, outfit, gadgets, and other equipment, it's time to test your superpowers. Even in the superhero world, practice makes perfect!

Your superpowers can help you fight baddies and keep you safe. Others might make it easier for you to move around and investigate. Some of them are just plain fun to use!

Not all superpowers are designed for fighting—sometimes you won't want to engage a bad guy. You'll need to be able to keep a baddie busy while you save some civilians or make a quick getaway.

Think about which superpowers would be best for different situations, and practice to make sure you are ready for anything!

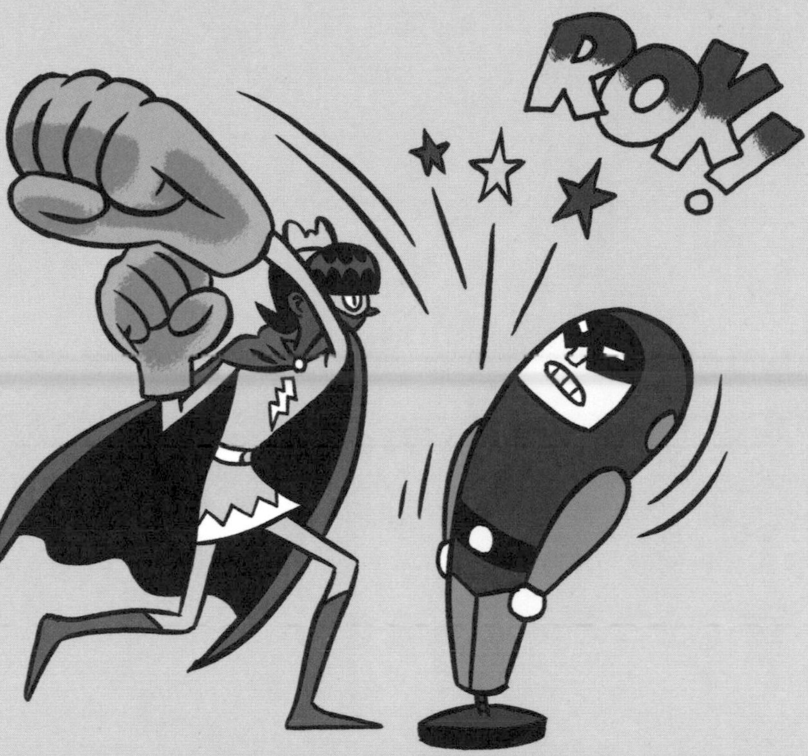
POW!

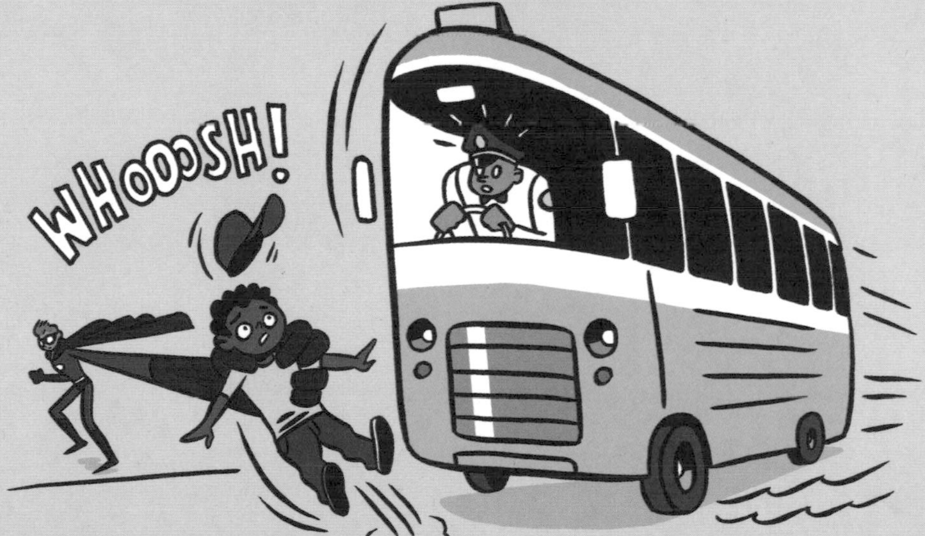
WHOOOSH!

MAKE YOURSELF
AS LIGHT AS A FEATHER

Test your super-stealth skills! To complete this task you need exceptional caution, incredible skill, and enormous self-control. You must make yourself as light as a feather!

MATERIALS

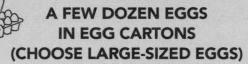

A FEW DOZEN EGGS
IN EGG CARTONS
(CHOOSE LARGE-SIZED EGGS)

A FEW LARGE
PLASTIC TRASH BAGS

DISINFECTANT

BUCKET OF SOAP AND WATER

  1 OR 2 SUPER SIDEKICKS

CRUNCH!

85

INSTRUCTIONS

1 Spread the trash bags out on the floor or outdoor area and place the egg cartons in two rows.

2 Check all the eggs to make sure there are no breaks or cracks in any of the eggshells. If you find any, replace the cracked eggs with new ones.

3 Make sure all the eggs are pointing the same way in the cartons. One end of the egg is more pointy, while the other end is more rounded. Just make sure that all of the eggs are oriented in the same direction—all the "pointy" ends up or all the rounded ends up. By doing this, your foot will have a more level surface on which to stand.

4 Now, take off your shoes and socks.

5 Locate one or two sidekicks to assist you as you step up onto the first carton of eggs. The key is to make your foot as flat as possible in order to distribute your weight evenly across the tops of the eggs. If the ball of your foot is large, try positioning it between two rows of eggs instead of resting it on top of an egg.

6 When your foot is properly positioned, gradually shift all of your weight onto that leg (the "egg-leg") as you position your other foot on top of the second carton of eggs. Your sidekicks can help you keep your balance.

7 You will hear creaking sounds coming from the egg carton, but don't get nervous. Ask the sidekicks to step away, and hey presto!

8 Now lift and place each foot carefully over the rows of eggs until you're back on solid ground. If you haven't cracked any eggs, then you've completed this activity perfectly. You're an eggs-cellent superhero!

9 Use the bucket of soap and water, and the disinfectant, to clean up any mess you have made.

SUPERHERO SECRET

The egg's unique shape gives it tremendous strength, even though it seems fragile. The egg is strongest at the top and the bottom. If you hold an egg in your hand and squeeze it on the top and the bottom, the egg doesn't break because you are adding pressure to the strongest parts of the shell. The curved form of the shell also distributes pressure evenly all over the shell rather than concentrating it at any one point.

HARNESS YOUR PSYCHOKINETIC POWERS

Sometimes being a superhero requires more than just physical strength. Use your super-smart superhero powers to crush a can without even having to touch it!

WARNING! This activity requires the use of a stove. All superheroes should have parental permission and supervision during this activity as your superpowers and a hot stove could combine to cause planet-wide chaos.

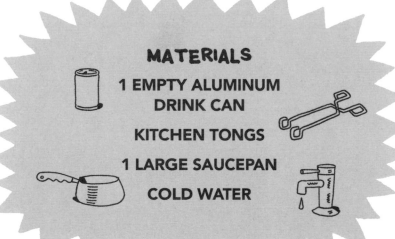

MATERIALS

1 EMPTY ALUMINUM DRINK CAN

KITCHEN TONGS

1 LARGE SAUCEPAN

COLD WATER

INSTRUCTIONS

1 Fill the saucepan with cold water.

2 Put a tablespoon of water inside the drink can.

3 Now heat the can on the stove to boil the water inside.

4 When the water is boiled, a little cloud of condensation will rise out of the top of the can.

5 Quickly and carefully use the tongs to lift the very hot can. Turn it completely upside down and place it in the saucepan of cold water.

KRUNCH!

6 Watch as the can is crushed immediately, right before your very eyes.

SUPERHERO SECRET

Heating the can caused the water inside it to boil. The water vapor from the boiling water forced the air inside the can out of it. Once the can was filled with water vapor and then suddenly cooled, the water vapor within the can condensed and created a vacuum. This vacuum inside the can made it easy for the pressure of the air outside the can to crush it without your help.

DEFY
GRAVITY

Your superhero skill is the key to defying gravity. It may take a little practice, but over time you will get better at playing with the forces of nature. Things normally fall from the sky, unless you are a bird or a plane or ... well, you know—but here you can reverse the normal force of gravity.

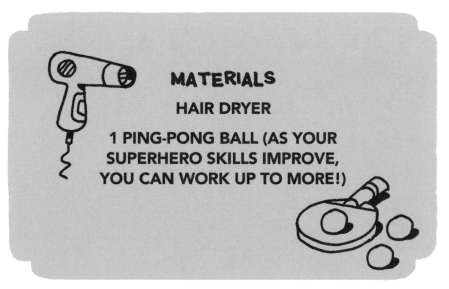

MATERIALS

HAIR DRYER

1 PING-PONG BALL (AS YOUR SUPERHERO SKILLS IMPROVE, YOU CAN WORK UP TO MORE!)

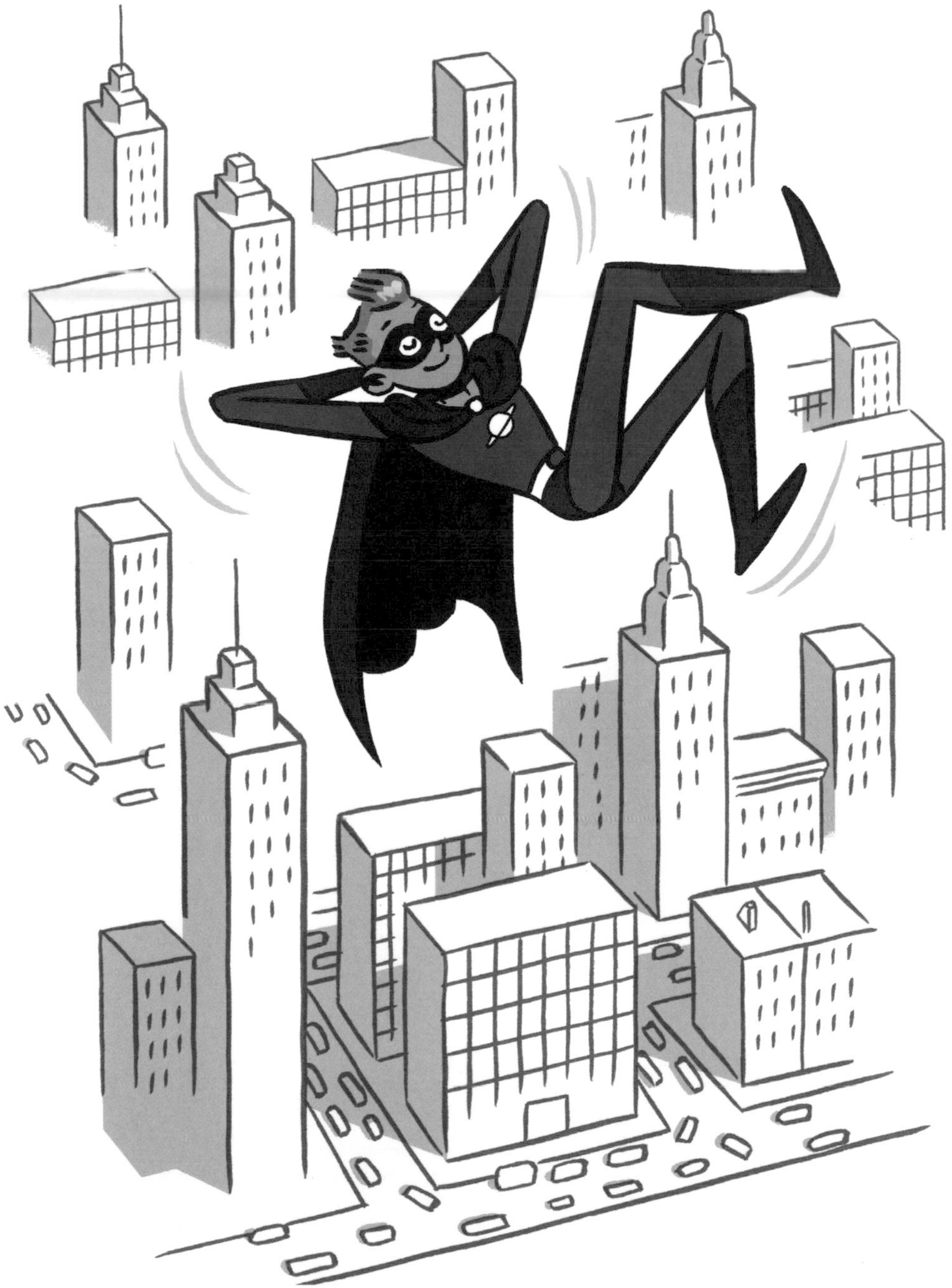

INSTRUCTIONS

1 Take the hair dryer and plug it in. Turn it on to the lowest and coolest setting.

2 Hold the hair dryer so that it is pointing straight up in the air.

3 Set your ping-pong ball directly above the current of air coming out of the hair dryer. What happens?

Once you have mastered defying gravity with one ball, practice until you can control two, three, or even more!

SUPERHERO SECRET

The moving hot air from the hair dryer pushes the ping-pong ball up with a force equal to the force of gravity. Also, air pressure creates a column of air in which the ping-pong ball is held, making it easier to control the movement of the ball. The tougher test is to control two, three, or even more ping-pong balls all at once. Practice will allow you to defy the force of gravity like a superhero!

TURN
BONES TO RUBBER

Some superheroes have the power to morph into any shape or bend their bodies in impossible ways. This activity takes a simple sturdy chicken bone and turns it into bendy rubber in front of your very eyes!

ZWOOOSH!

MATERIALS

1 CONTAINER OR BEAKER

1 UNCOOKED CHICKEN BONE

VINEGAR

PAPER TOWELS

INSTRUCTIONS

1 Clean and dry the chicken bone with the paper towels. It is best to leave it to dry overnight.

2 Place the bone in the container.

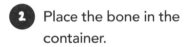

3 Take the vinegar and fill the container until the bone is completely covered.

Now, you have to use super patience and wait: leave the bone in the solution for six or seven days. What do you find?

The acid in the vinegar works to dissolve the calcium in the chicken bone—the calcium is what makes bones strong and rigid. Once this has been dissolved away all that is left is soft, flexible material that is super bendable.

MAKE A
SUPERHERO
WHIRLWIND

Some superheroes have perfected the art of spinning around on one spot so fast that they use it as a way to change from their alter ego into their superhero identity in a flash. Others can move at such great speeds that they are faster than the naked eye can see. With this activity, you too can create a super whirlwind—but with a little glitter you can see it spinning!

MATERIALS

1 SEE-THROUGH PLASTIC BOTTLE WITH A SCREW-ON CAP

1 TUBE OF GLITTER

WASHING-UP LIQUID

TAP WATER

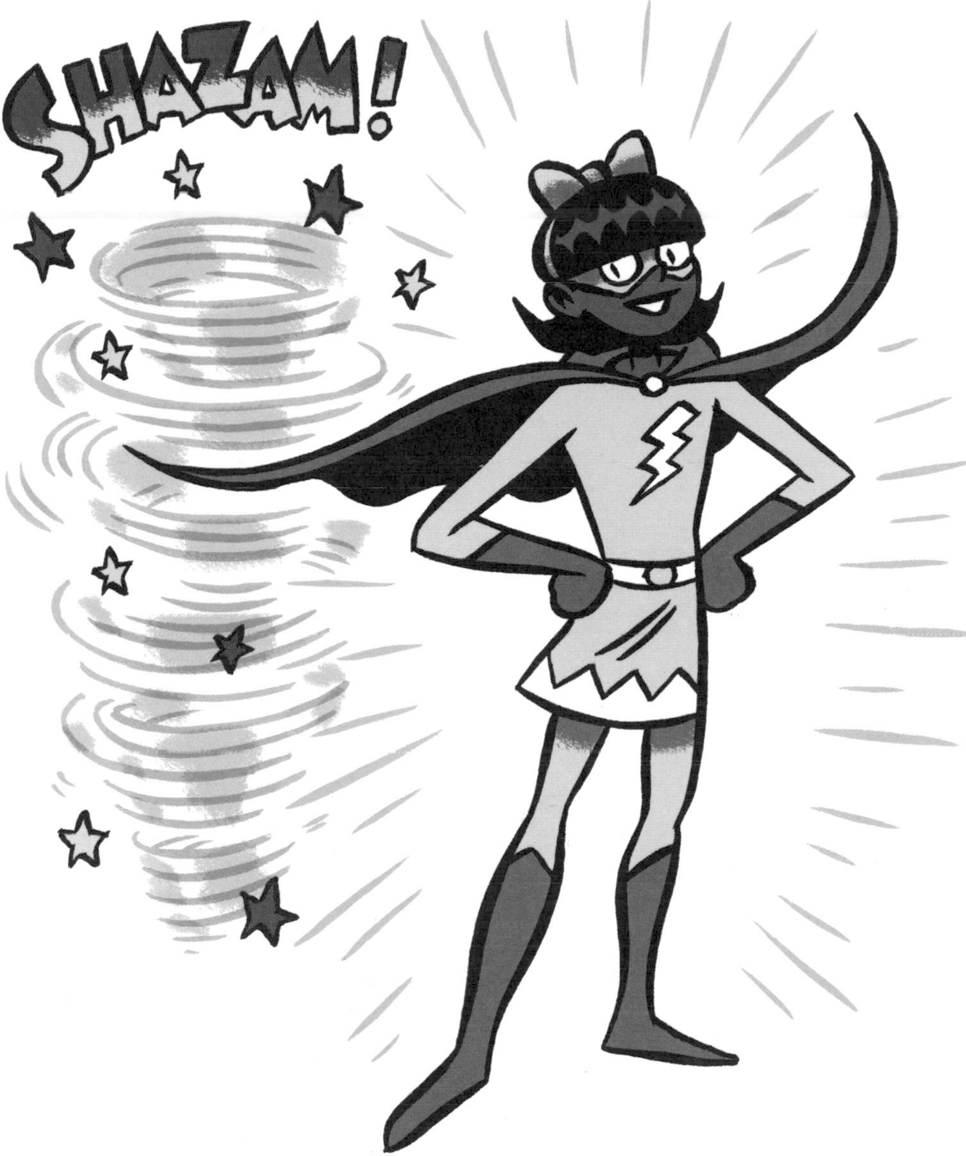
SHAZAM!

INSTRUCTIONS

1 Add water to your see-through bottle until it's about three-quarters full.

2 Drop in one or two squirts of washing-up liquid.

3 Now drop in some glitter.

4 Screw the cap on to your bottle.

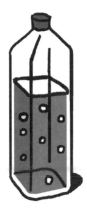

5 Hold your bottle upside down and shake it round and round in a circular movement. What do you see?

SUPERHERO SECRET

Shaking the bottle in a circular motion sets up a spinning force or vortex just like those superhero spins—the glitter you added makes it easier for you to track the motion of the water. It is these types of forces that create real-life spinning storms like tornadoes.

CONTROL A
FORCE OF
NATURE

Nature is one of the most powerful forces in the universe.
Even the strongest superhero can find it difficult to stop
nature in its tracks, but with practice it can be done.
Water can spill everywhere, but this activity will teach
you how to use super precision and skill to keep the
water under your control.

MATERIALS

WATER

ZIP-SEAL SANDWICH BAGS

SHARP PENCILS

A SINK

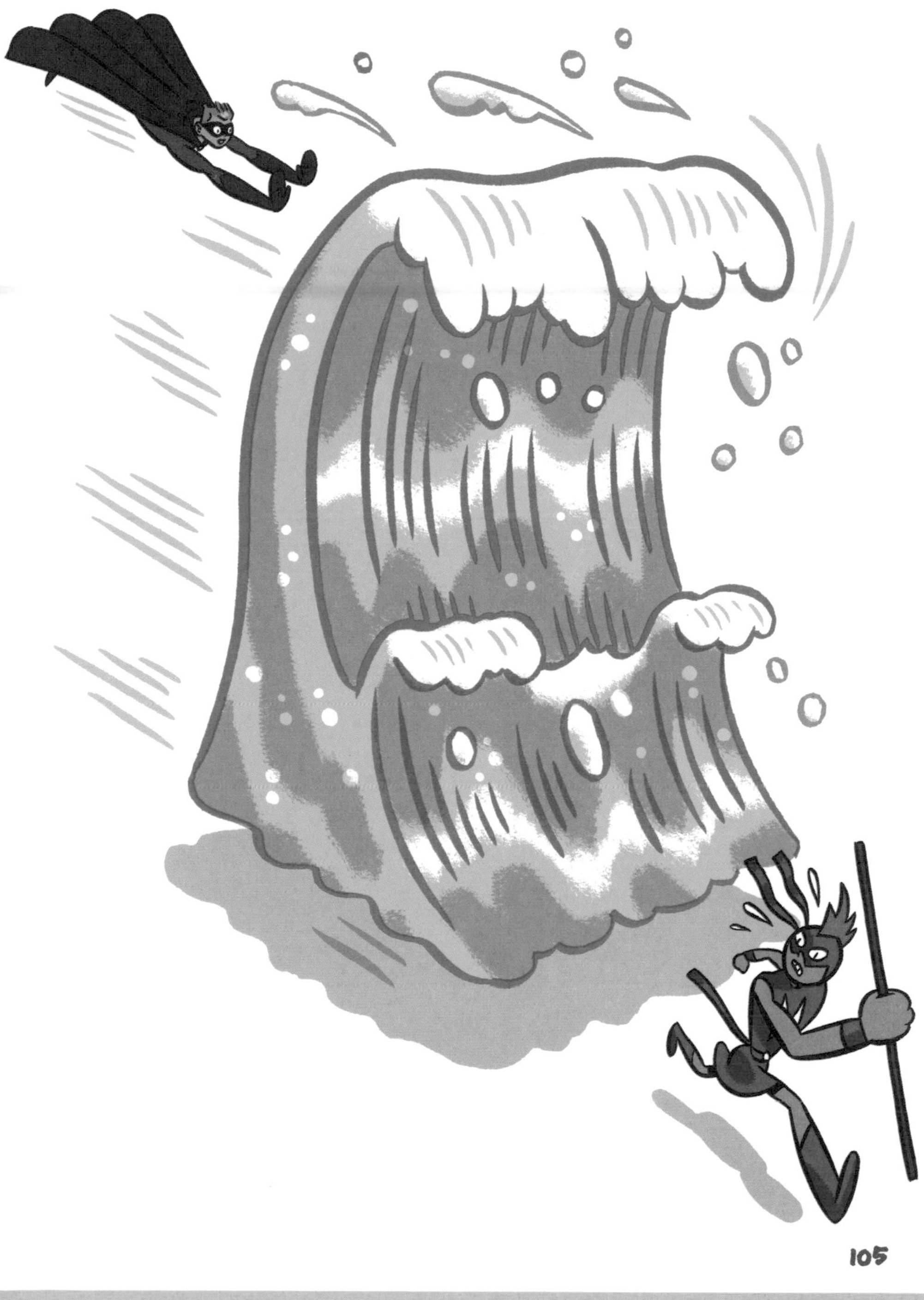

INSTRUCTIONS

1. Fill a sandwich bag with water to about half full, then seal it with the zip.

2. Take a sharp pencil and pierce the bag. Continue to push it carefully through until it comes through the other side. Do not push the pencil any further after this or you'll spring a leak.

3 Repeat with other pencils, several times.

4 If you haven't pushed the pencil too far, then you will have successfully left this bag well and truly pierced without any spills. Your bag should look like something that has got on the wrong side of a superhero! When finished, remove the pencils over the sink.

SUPERHERO SECRET

Plastic bags are made from polymers—long chains of molecules that are super flexible and give the bag its stretchiness. When the sharp pencil pokes through the bag, the stretchy plastic hugs the pencil, creating a watertight seal around it ... and the bag doesn't leak. Amazing!

DISTRACT
YOUR ENEMY

Sometimes a direct attack is not the best move. Deploy these devices at just the right moment to create a noisy diversion and distract your enemy, giving you time to save some civilians or make a quick getaway!

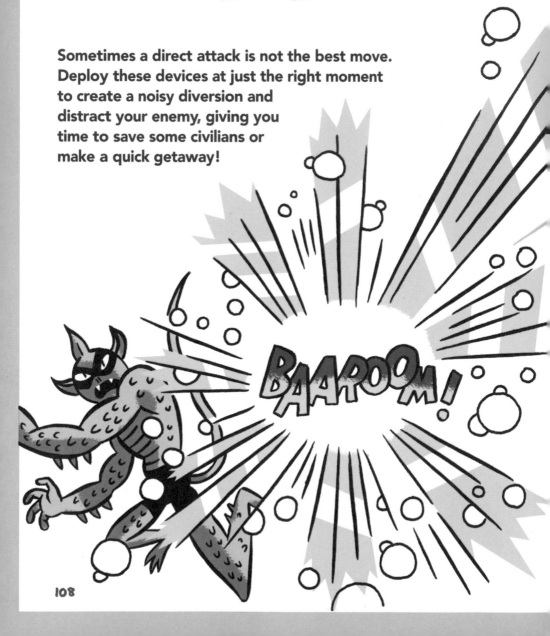

WARNING! This activity is messy and is probably best done outdoors, in a bathtub, or in your secret laboratory.

MATERIALS
VINEGAR
BAKING SODA
1 MEASURING CUP
WARM WATER
PAPER TOWELS OR TISSUES
1 ZIP-SEAL FREEZER BAG

INSTRUCTIONS

1 Place a couple of teaspoons of baking soda in the middle of a paper towel or a tissue. Fold the edges of the tissue over so that the baking soda is held in a little square.

2 Pour 4 fl oz of vinegar and 2 fl oz of warm water into the zip-seal freezer bag.

3 Next, you need to work fast. Zip the freezer bag closed as far as you can before finally allowing the tissue with baking soda to fall into the bag. Zip the remainder of the bag shut then place it or throw it at the bad guys and move fast!

● Watch from a distance.
The freezer bag should begin
to inflate before it goes BANG!,
creating a super diversion!

When the vinegar is absorbed into
the tissue, it mixes with the baking
soda. This causes a chemical reaction
that creates a lot of carbon dioxide gas.
The problem is that the gas needs space
to spread out and there simply isn't enough
room in the zip-seal bag, which means the
bag quickly inflates and then—BANG!—
it explodes.

SUPERHERO
CERTIFICATE

THIS IS TO CERTIFY THAT

_____

(WRITE YOUR SUPERHERO NAME HERE)

HAS COMPLETED TRAINING AND IS NOW A FULLY QUALIFIED SUPERHERO, READY TO FIGHT THE FORCES OF EVIL, DEFEND THE INNOCENT FROM INJUSTICE, AND UPHOLD THE VALUES OF COURAGE, HONESTY, LOYALTY, AND AWESOMENESS.

B.L.A.S.T

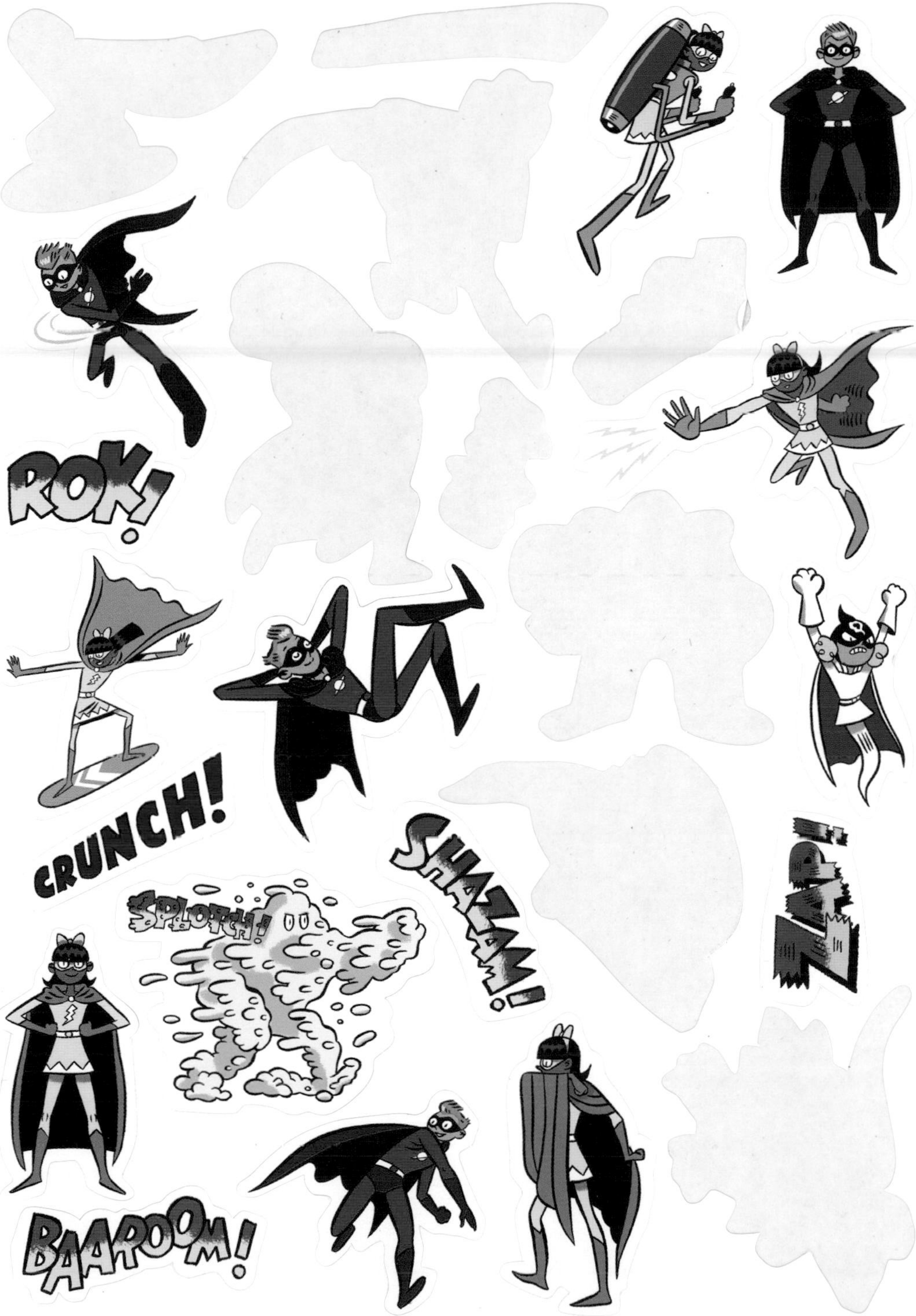
ROK!
CRUNCH!
SHAZAM!
ZAP!
SPLORCH!
BAAROOM!